NELSON MANDELA
Freedom for South Africa

NELSON MANDELA
Freedom for South Africa

By Pamela Dell

CHILDRENS PRESS ®
CHICAGO

PHOTO CREDITS

Cover: © Paula Bronstein/Impact Visuals
AP/Wide World: 3, 5, 14, 15, 16, 17, 21
Impact Visuals: © Eli Weinberg/IDAF: 1, 11, 18
      © Kuninori Takahashi: 2, 30
      © Auf Derhyd/Afrapix: 9
      © Anna Zieminski/Afrapix: 29
© Jason Lauré: 7, 12, 13
Reuters/Bettmann Newsphotos: 25, 27, 28, 31, 32

EDITORIAL STAFF

Project Editor: Mark Friedman
Design and Electronic Composition: Biner Design
Photo Editor: Jan Izzo

Library of Congress Cataloging-in-Publication Data
Dell, Pamela.
    Nelson Mandela : freedom for South Africa / by Pamela
Dell.
      p. cm. — (Picture story biography)
    ISBN 0-516-04192-4
    1. Mandela, Nelson, 1918-   —Juvenile literature.
2. Presidents—South Africa—Biography—Juvenile
literature. 3. South Africa—Politics and government—
1989-   —Juvenile literature. I. Title. II. Series: Picture-story
biographies.

DT1949.M35D45 1994   94-3386
968.06′4′092—dc20   CIP
[B]   AC

Nelson Mandela smiles after being elected South Africa's president.

IN MAY 1994, a great wave of hope swept over South Africa. For the first time in that country's troubled history, a black man had been elected to the highest office. His name was Nelson Rolihlahla Mandela.

Mandela was nearly 75 years old at the time of his election. Only four years earlier he had been released from prison, where he had spent 27 terrible years. Yet now, on the day he was sworn in as South Africa's first black president, he stood tall, vigorous, and joyous in victory.

Mandela stood before a crowd of thousands and raised his clenched fist. The gesture was a symbol of the long and bitter fight he and his followers had waged to defeat the racist government of South Africa. For decades, many people thought this victory would be impossible.

Hundreds of years of racial hatred had robbed the South African black people of freedom, civil rights, and political power. The white South African policy of "apartheid," or apartness, had kept non-white South Africans segregated from whites for decades. When Hendrik F. Verwoerd became prime minister of South Africa in 1958, he and others in Parliament acted on their belief that whites were the most civilized race. They thought that black Africans, Asians, and other "colored" people were lesser races, and they should be forced into lower positions in society.

The laws of apartheid kept blacks separated from whites in virtually all areas of South African life.

In the 1940s, the all-white Parliament began passing the laws of apartheid. The government severely restricted the voting rights of non-whites. It passed laws that limited the quality of the education and jobs that blacks could receive. The entire South African economy was structured to favor white-owned businesses. This forced non-white citizens into unemployment and poverty. The government uprooted native Africans from their longtime homes and forced them into rural territories or townships. Living conditions in the townships were repulsive.

Through years of injustice and imprisonment, Nelson Mandela maintained his dignity. He never stopped believing that all people everywhere deserved to be free from government oppression.

Nelson Rolihlahla Mandela was born on July 18, 1918, in a tiny place known as Mvezo. He was given the tribal name of *Rolihlahla*. This is Mandela's true name. Later, when he attended a Methodist grammar school run by missionaries, he began to be called Nelson. In the Thembu language, Rolihlahla means "to stir up trouble" or "to bring trouble upon oneself." But Rolihlahla was an obedient and respectful child who did not cause trouble.

Soon after he was born, the family moved to the village of Qunu, near Umtata. Umtata is the capital of what is now the independent black homeland of Transkei. Rolihlahla belonged to a highly distinguished tribal family. His great-great-grandfather had been a famous Transkeian king. His father, Henry, was an important leader in the Thembu tribe, part of the larger Xhosa tribe.

Qunu, where Nelson Mandela spent his early childhood

When Rolihlahla was only ten, his
father became ill and passed away.
Rolihlahla was sent to live in the village
of Mqekezweni with his uncle, Chief
Jongintaba. Mqekezweni was known as
the "Great Place" because it was the
village where all important tribal
business occurred.

Even as a boy, Rolihlahla was
fascinated by the political process and
the affairs of his people. He loved to
listen when the elders gathered to tell
stories. They told tales about their days
of freedom before the white Europeans
came to their land. They talked of the
mighty warriors who had battled the
whites to defend the tribes of Africa.

By the time Nelson Mandela was in
college, he was a tall, good-humored
young man. His laugh came easily, and
he was highly intelligent. But he did not
like injustice of any kind. During his
second year of college, he participated in

As a young man, Nelson Mandela was an excellent athlete.

a student strike to protest the poor conditions at school. When he refused to apologize to the school authorities, he was expelled. This was Nelson's first real experience of standing up against authority.

Many South African whites lived a luxurious lifestyle (right), while almost all non-whites were forced to live in poverty in the townships (opposite page).

After being expelled from school, Nelson made his way to Johannesburg, the "City of Gold." At first sight, Johannesburg may have seemed like a wonderful place. It was a wealthy city, thriving on its successful gold-mining industry. But the nice parks, theaters, and schools were only for the use of the white residents. Like all other Johannesburg blacks, Nelson was forced to live in a township on the outskirts of

the city. There, almost nobody had adequate plumbing, electricity, indoor toilets, or even garbage collection. The air smelled of raw sewage. Men and women were required to live many miles from their jobs. Most people barely had enough money for bus fare to work.

Nelson was determined to return to college and become a lawyer so that he could try and change his society for the better. He began taking courses at the

University of Witwatersrand. He also married a young woman named Evelyn Ntoko Mase; the couple eventually had three children.

Mandela's hatred for life under a racist government grew rapidly. By the late 1940s, he was living up to his tribal name of Rolihlahla — he became skilled at "bringing trouble upon himself" in the name of freedom. He joined the African National Congress (ANC), a political party formed by blacks to fight for equal rights and protest apartheid. Mandela

Mandela in his early days as a leader of the African National Congress

Mandela in the law office he opened with Oliver Tambo

and his close friends, Oliver Tambo and Walter Sisulu, formed the ANC Youth League in 1944 to communicate an even more focused message.

In 1952, the government issued its first of several "bans" on Mandela. For several years, Nelson had organized labor strikes, written articles, and delivered speeches to thousands of people. When he was banned, the police ordered Mandela to stay away from meetings of more than three people. He was also not allowed to leave Johannesburg. But Nelson did continue his work as a lawyer and pushed forward with his anti-apartheid protests.

In December 1956, the police broke into Mandela's home in the middle of the night and arrested him. He and dozens of others were put on trial for treason, or betraying the government.

Nelson was free on bail during his four-year trial, but his movement and activities were severely limited. The trial caused tremendous strain in Mandela's private life. His political involvement had previously led to divorce in his first marriage. At the time of his trial, his

The government arrested Mandela for giving speeches like this, in which he encouraged blacks to break the laws of apartheid.

Nelson (right) goes to court with fellow defendants Robert Resha (left) and Patrick Molaoa.

second wife, Winnie (Winifred Madikizela), had to cope with the worry that Nelson might be convicted and sent to prison.

In August 1961, the verdict was finally read. Though Mandela was still banned, he was found not guilty and was set free. Although he won his case, Mandela realized he could not operate

Mandela defie
South African
government a
prepares to bu
identification
passbook. Apa
laws required
to carry these
passbooks.

ANC activities while under the government ban. So he decided to go "underground." He went into hiding, and only his most trusted associates knew his location. It was a tremendous sacrifice that meant he would only see Winnie and their two daughters during brief secret meetings.

Mandela soon became known as "the Black Pimpernel," a nickname based on a novel about the French Revolution called *The Scarlet Pimpernel*. In the novel, a man eludes the police by dressing in disguises and hiding in secret places. Mandela had similar methods. He disguised himself as a laborer, janitor, or chauffeur. Even though he was one of the most powerful leaders of the ANC, he had the ability to take on a disguise and disappear in a crowd. For more than a year underground, Mandela managed to elude the police and continue pushing forward with his fight against the government. He even managed to travel to other African countries and Great Britain to obtain support, military training, and funding for the ANC.

In 1962, Mandela formed *Umkhonto we Sizwe* — the "spear of the nation." This organization was the militant wing of the ANC. Mandela had studied the principles of Mahatma Gandhi, the great leader of India. For years, he had tried to follow Gandhi's method of peaceful resistance. But this strategy had failed in South Africa. Mandela now believed the only way he could fight the brutal South African government was to resort to violence. So members of Umkhonto we Sizwe were trained in armed combat and taught how to build bombs. Though Mandela and his followers wanted to spare human life wherever possible, some people were inevitably injured or killed in ensuing conflicts.

On August 5, 1962, Mandela was going to Johannesburg disguised as a chauffeur. Someone had apparently informed the police of his true identity. The police stopped Mandela and arrested him. Mandela was charged with illegally leaving the country and with "incitement," or stirring up trouble.

*A grim Mandela
goes to court.*

After a three-month trial, an all-white jury found Mandela guilty. The court sentenced him to five years in prison, and he was immediately taken to Pretoria Central Prison. To protest his imprisonment, Mandela refused to eat or to change into prison clothing. As punishment, he was put in solitary confinement for two months.

In a cell all alone, Mandela nearly went mad. He had no one to talk to and nothing to read. He sat on the dirt floor in darkness. He was only allowed out of his cell for half an hour a day. At last, in order to survive, Mandela gave in. He agreed to eat the awful prison food and accepted prison clothes. He had given in to the authorities on these points, but in his heart, he was more committed than ever to defy them.

Prison officials transferred Mandela and many other political prisoners to the stone prison fortress on Robben Island, off the coast of Cape Town. The guards there forced Mandela to perform hard labor. Every day, he spent hours under the blazing sun pounding stones into gravel in the island quarry. Every aspect of prison life was devised to increase the prisoners' suffering. The guards did not allow Mandela to wear shoes or a shirt at work in the quarry. And they cut off his contact with the outside world: no visitors, letters, or books were allowed.

During this first sentence, Mandela suffered a further legal setback. The government had seized many important ANC documents that revealed how Mandela and others had attempted to destroy apartheid through violence. The government brought a new case against the ANC leaders. Mandela went on trial once again. In June 1964, he was found guilty. Mandela and nine others were sentenced to life imprisonment.

So Mandela returned to prison wondering if he would ever be free. Even worse, he could not help his wife and children, who were being watched and harassed by the police. Winnie Mandela was arrested and imprisoned for more than a year as a result of her own political activities.

Meanwhile, Nelson continued to study in prison, and he took it upon himself to educate the younger prisoners. Because of his influence on his fellow inmates,

Robben Island became known as "Mandela University." And although he was behind bars, he was perhaps an even stronger inspiration to the downtrodden people of South Africa. Mandela proclaimed, "The struggle is my life. I will continue to fight for freedom until the end of my days."

His words were eventually heard around the world. People everywhere grew outraged over the situation in South Africa and began petitioning their governments to take action. The "Free Mandela" campaign spread to all corners of the globe. Not only did people want Mandela freed, but they called for an end to apartheid. In the 1970s, the United Nations instituted an arms embargo against South Africa. The United States Congress passed a law that cut off virtually all U.S. business dealings with South Africa. Many other nations followed this example. These

Protesters in South Africa and around the world lobbied for the release of Mandela.

economic "sanctions" were intended to damage the South African economy and force the South African government to reform its racist policies.

In 1982, Mandela and other major ANC figures were moved to Pollsmoor Prison, where conditions were not as brutal as at Robben Island. The government, now headed by Prime

Minister P. W. Botha, repealed several apartheid laws, including the requirement that blacks must carry identity passes wherever they went. But partial change was not enough. Black Africans were nearing the point of all-out revolt. Labor strikes and violent protests grew, and the government declared a state of emergency. The police engaged blacks in savage battles that cost hundreds of lives. The government also censored the press to stop the world from seeing these horrible events.

By 1985, the government realized the country was falling apart. It decided to let Mandela go free if he would denounce the violent actions of the ANC. The government wanted to negotiate with Mandela. But Mandela refused to grant them the opportunity, saying, "Only free men can negotiate." He *chose* to remain a prisoner. His message was that even if he were freed into a society still ruled by apartheid, he and all black South Africans would still be prisoners.

In 1988, Mandela endured a bout of tuberculosis that nearly claimed his life. He was then moved to the Victor Verster Prison, where he was allowed to live in a relatively comfortable house. Still, it was prison. He was now being visited by important government officials, including the new South African president, Frederick Willem de Klerk. Mandela gradually became convinced that de Klerk was serious about dismantling all aspects of apartheid.

Mandela spent the last years of his prison sentence at this house in the Victor Verster Prison.

At 4:15 P.M. on the historic day of February 11, 1990, Nelson Mandela at last walked out of prison a free man. His long-held demands had been met by President de Klerk. He walked down a dirt road to the gate of the prison. He smiled to the gathered crowd and raised his clenched fist, the symbol of his continuing struggle. Television cameras showed pictures of one of the most powerful men in the world, but one who had not been seen in public for 27 years.

After nearly three decades in prison, a joyous Mandela walks out into freedom with wife Winnie at his side.

Mandela's release from prison touched off celebrations across South Africa.

The jubilation that burst forth in South Africa on that February day faded quickly. Mandela's freedom had come, but the final end to apartheid was a slower process. Mandela and de Klerk held intensive discussions on how to reform the South African government. For their efforts in bringing change, Mandela and de Klerk were both awarded the Nobel Peace Prize on October 15, 1993.

Finally, in November 1993, a new national consititution was adopted. The next step to completing this revolution was a presidential election, which was held in the last week of April 1994. Millions of black Africans voted for the first time in their lives. When the votes were tallied the following week, Nelson Mandela's election was finally announced.

It was the pinnacle moment in Mandela's long, heroic life. When he took power from F. W. de Klerk,

Mandela casts a vote for himself for president of South Africa.

South Africa's new president, Nelson Mandela, celebrates with former president F. W. de Klerk as Mandela is inaugurated on May 10, 1994.

President Nelson Mandela proved that his years of captivity had not been in vain.

Many people fight daily to uphold their beliefs. A few find the courage and strength to continue their fight even when they are hunted, beaten down, imprisoned, thrown into darkness, and silenced. Nelson Rolihlahla Mandela is one of those few. His name will never be forgotten.

Nelson Mandela

1918	July 18 — Nelson Rolihlahla Mandela is born
1930	After the death of his father, Nelson begins living with his uncle, chief of the Thembu
1938	Begins college education
1940	Expelled from college for participating in a student strike
1941	Begins studying law in Johannesburg
1942	Graduates from University of Witwatersrand and becomes a lawyer
1944	Forms African National Congress (ANC) Youth League
1952	Arrested for breaking curfew; "banned" by the government for the first time
1956	Arrested and put on trial
1961	Mandela's trial ends with his acquittal; he goes underground
1962	Arrested again and sentenced to five years in prison
1964	Tried again for treason, sentenced to life in prison
1990	February 11 — released from prison
1994	Elected president of South Africa

Index

(**bold-face type** indicates photographs)

African National Congress (ANC), 14, 18, 19, 20, 23, 25, 26
ANC Youth League, 15
apartheid, 6, 7, 15, 24, 26, 27, 29
Black Pimpernel, the, 19
Botha, P. W., 26
Cape Town, South Africa, 22
Chief Jongintaba (uncle), 10
De Klerk, Frederick Willem, 27, 28, 29, 30, **31**
economic sanctions, 25
"Free Mandela" campaign, 24
Gandhi, Mahatma, 20
Great Britain, 19
Johannesburg, South Africa, 12, 15, 20
Mandela, Henry (father), 9, 10

Mandela, Nelson, **1, 3, 5, 6, 11, 14, 15, 16, 17, 18, 21, 28, 30, 31**
  banned by government, 15, 17
  birth, 8
  childhood, 8–10
  education, 10, 11, 13–14
  elected president, 5, 30
  marriages, 14, 16–17
  name, 8–9, 14
  prison, 5, 21–22, 23-24, 25–27, 28
  protesting apartheid, 10–11
  trials, 16, 21, 23
  tuberculosis, 27
  underground, 18
Mandela, Winnie (second wife), 17, 23, **28**
Mase, Evelyn Ntoko (first wife), 14
Mqekezweni, South Africa, 10
Mvezo, South Africa, 8
Nobel Peace Prize, 29

Parliament, 6, 7
Pollsmoor Prison, 25
Pretoria Central Prison, 21
Qunu, South Africa, 9, **9**
Robben Island, 22, 24, 25
Scarlet Pimpernel, The, 19
Sisulu, Walter, 15
Tambo, Oliver, 9, 15
Thembu (tribe), 8, 9
townships, 12–13, **13**
Transkei, South Africa, 9
Umkhonto we Sizwe, 19–20
Umtata, South Africa, 9
United Nations, 24
United States Congress, 24
University of Witwatersrand, 14
Verwoerd, Hendrik F., 6
Victor Verster Prison, 27
Xhosa (tribe), 9

About the Author

Pamela Dell was born in Idaho, grew up in Chicago, and now lives in Santa Monica, California. At the age of five she decided she should be a writer and began writing stories. In sixth grade, she joined forces with a friend and published her own magazine. Since that encouraging beginning, she has worked as a writer and editor in many different fields and has published nonfiction and short fiction for both adult and young adult readers. She is also the author of the Childrens Press Picture-Story Biographies *Michael Chang: Tennis Champion* and *I. M. Pei: Designer of Dreams.*